A 3-minute forever book

EAT
YOUR
PEAS™

for Someone Special

By Cheryl Karpen
Gently Spoken

A gift for

_Shelley_

from

_Shara_

You are a
very special someone
and
I wanted to let you know
how important you are to me.

May the words in this book
remind you often.

At the heart of this little book
is a promise.
It's a promise from me to you
and it goes like this:

If you ever need someone to talk to,
someone to listen
- really listen -
to what's on your mind
and in your heart
just tap on my shoulder,
knock on my door
or give me a call.

I'll be there for you
when you want to
shout for joy in celebration

or when you simply
need a shoulder to lean on.

What's more, I promise
to try and lift you up
and never let you down.

In the meantime,
here are a few things
I'd like you to
know,
remember,
**take to heart,**
and never, ever doubt.

Whenever you come to mind
I see a
remarkable,
loving,
generous,
compassionate,
kind
and wonderful you!

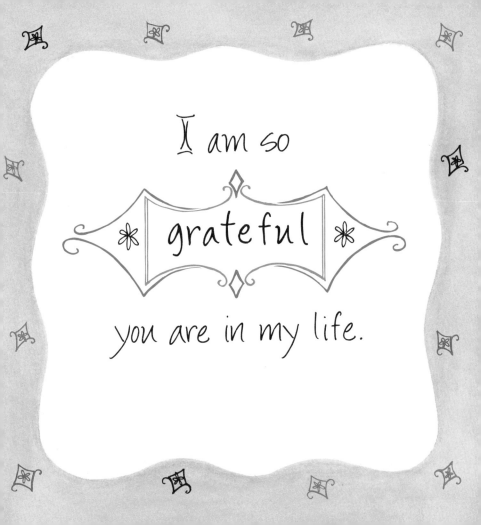

I admire you for your

strength

wisdom

courage

There's nobody else like you.

Anywhere.  Anyplace.

Your presence in my life
is
truly
a special gift.

Thank you for the times you have been there for me.

I cannot imagine
being without
your grace
to cheer me on.

I want to always
be there for you, too.

I appreciate you.

Each new sunrise is a reminder that
every day
is a
new beginning.

Dream big dreams.

Imagine yourself
in places you've never been before.

Hear applause.

# Why wait?

Sing more
Dance more
Play more
Laugh more
Dream more
Learn more
Love more
Imagine more!

Be true to yourself.

It's one of the greatest gifts you can give.

To anyone. Anywhere. Anytime.

I believe in you.

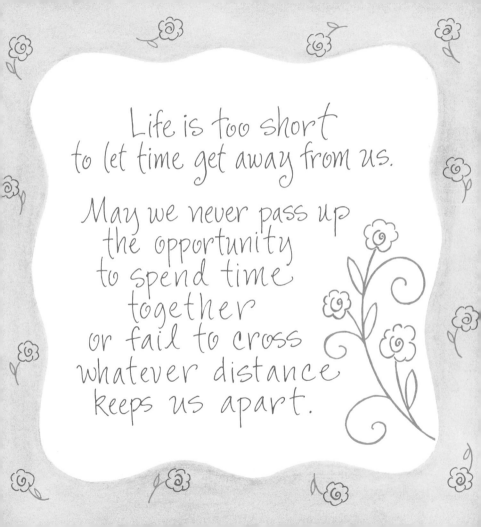

Life is too short
to let time get away from us.

May we never pass up
the opportunity
to spend time
together
or fail to cross
whatever distance
keeps us apart.

Keep this little book
where you can see it often
so it will remind you
of the place
you hold in my heart.

Remember my promise.
I will always be there for you.

to help celebrate your
courage,

to champion your
dreams,

and to remind you to
stay healthy ...

Remember to eat your peas!

## Why Peas?

She was a vibrant, dazzling young woman with a promising future.
Yet, at sixteen, her world felt sad and hopeless.

I was living over 1800 miles away and wanted to let this very special young person in my life know I would be there for her across the miles and through the darkness. I wanted her to know she could call me any time, at any hour, and I would be there for her. And I wanted to give her a piece of my heart she could take with her anywhere—a reminder she was loved.
Really loved.

Her name is Maddy and she was the inspiration for my first PEAS book, Eat Your Peas for Young Adults. At the very beginning of her book I made a place to write in my phone number so she knew I was serious about being available. And right beside the phone number I put my promise to listen—really listen—whenever that call came.

Soon after the book was published, people began to ask me if I had the same promise and affirmation for adults. I realized it isn't just young people who need to be reminded how truly special they are. We all do.

Today Maddy is thriving and giving hope to others in her life. If someone has given you this book, it means you are pretty special to them and they wanted to let you know. Take it to heart.

Believe it, and remind yourself often.

Wishing you peas and plenty of joy,

Cheryl Karpen

P.S. My Mama always said, "Eat Your Peas, they're good for you."
The pages of this book are filled with nutrients for the heart.
They're simply good for you too.

A portion of the profits from the
Eat Your Peas Collection
will benefit empowerment programs
for youth and adults.

My
sincerest gratitude
to all the
"Someone Specials"
who grace our
lives with their kindness.

You know who you are.

Blessings,

*Cheryl*

Cheryl Karpen

If this book has touched your life,
we'd love to hear your story.
Please send it to:
mystory@eatyourpeas.com
or mail it to:
Gently Spoken
PO Box 365
St. Francis, MN 55070

## About the author

"Eat Your Peas"

A self-proclaimed dreamer, Cheryl
spends her time imagining and creating
between the historic river town of Anoka, Minnesota
and the seaside village of Islamorada, Florida.

An effervescent speaker, Cheryl brings inspiration,
insight, and humor to corporations,
professional organizations and churches.
Learn more about her at www.cherylkarpen.com

## About the illustrator

Sandy Fougner artfully weaves
a love for design, illustration and
interiors with being a wife
and mother of three sons.

Other books by Cheryl Karpen

## The Eat Your Peas Collection™

is now available in the following titles:

Mothers
Fathers
Daughters
Grandkids
Sisters
Daughter-in-law
New Moms
Faithfully

Girlfriends
Sons
Birthdays
For the Cure
Tough Times
Extraordinary
    Young Person

New titles are SPROUTING up all the time!

## Heart and Soul Collection
Hope for a Hurting Heart
Can We Try Again? Finding a way back to love

For more inspiration, Like us on Facebook at the **Eat Your Peas Collection**.
For quotes and pages to post, follow us on Pinterest at
www.pinterest.com/eatyourpeasbook/

To view a complete collection, visit us online at www.eatyourpeas.com

# Eat Your Peas® for Someone Special

©2005, Cheryl Karpen
New Edition, November 2017

Home grown in the USA

For more information or to locate a store near you, contact:

Gently Spoken
PO Box 365
St. Francis, MN 55070

Toll-free 1-877-224-7886 or visit us online at
www.eatyourpeas.com